newwoman

Bloke jokes

A CIP catalogue for this book is available from the British Library.

ISBN 1 84222 090 X

Art Direction: Diane Spender
Editor: Louise Johnson
Production: Garry Lewis
Illustrations: Sarah Nayler

INDEX

Newwoman

Edited by **Louise Johnson**

Bloke Jokes

...because men are funny

CONTENTS

1

WHAT'S THE DIFFERENCE, ANYWAY......

What's the **difference** between a **bloke** and a **pig**?

A pig doesn't turn into a bloke after two pints of lager!

What's the difference between hard and dark?

It stays dark all night.

What's the **difference** between a **bloke** and a **shopping trolley**?

Sometimes a shopping trolley has a mind of its own.

What's the difference between a bloke and childbirth?

One can be terribly painful and sometimes almost unbearable while the other is only having a baby.

What's the difference between a bloke and a bloke's photo?

The photo is fully developed.

What's the difference between a bar and a clitoris?

Most blokes have no trouble finding a bar.

What's the difference between a bloke and a computer?

You only have to punch the information into a computer once.

What's the difference between a woman and a computer?

A computer doesn't laugh at a 3.5-inch floppy.

What's the difference between an attractive man and an ugly man?

About 10 glasses of wine.

What is the difference between your husband and your lover?

About four hours.

What's the difference between light and hard?

A bloke can sleep with a light on.

What's the difference between a bloke
and a piece of cheese?

Cheese matures.

What's the **difference** between a **golf ball** and a **G-spot**?

Men will always look for a golf ball.

What's the difference between single women and married women?

Single women go home, see what's in the fridge then
go to bed. Married women go home, see what's in
the bed then go to the fridge!

What's the **difference** between a **porcupine** and a **sports car**?

A porcupine has pricks on the outside.

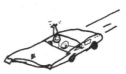

What's the difference between *Match Of The Day* and the toilet seat?

A bloke never will never miss *Match Of The Day*.

What's the difference between a bloke and a battery?

A battery has a positive side!

What's the difference between a single 40-year-old woman and a single 40-year-old bloke?

The 40-year-old woman often thinks of having children and the 40-year-old bloke often thinks about dating them.

What's the **difference** between a **new husband** and a **new dog**?

After a year, the dog is still excited to see you.

2

EVERYONE LIKES A LIST, DON'T THEY...

Seminars For Men

- Combating Stupidity.
- Understanding Your Financial Incompetence.

Reasons To Give Flowers

- How To Stay Awake After Sex.
- Why The Weekend And Sports Are Not Synonymous.
- The Morning Dilemma – If It's Awake, Take A Shower?
- Helpful Postural Hints For Couch Potatoes.
- How Not To Act Younger Than Your Children.
- The Remote Control – Overcoming Your Dependency.

- How To Take Illness Like An Adult.
- You – The Weaker Sex.
- P.M.S. – Learning When To Keep Your Mouth Shut.
- You Too Can Do Housework.
- How To Fill An Ice Cube Tray.
- We Do Not Want Sleazy Underthings For Christmas
    – Give Us Money.

Wonderful Laundry Techniques (formerly called 'Don't Wash My Silks').

- Understanding The Female Response To Your
  Coming In Drunk At 4a.m.
- Parenting – No, It Doesn't End With Conception.
- Get A Life – Learn How To Cook.
- How Not To Act Like An Idiot When You Are
  Obviously Wrong.

Why blokes are like computers
- They have a lot of data but are still clueless.
- A better model is always just around the corner.
- They look nice and shiny until you bring them home.
- It's always necessary to have a back-up.
- They'll do whatever you say if you push the right buttons.
- The best part of having one is the games you can play.
- They get hot when you turn them on – and that's the only
  time you get their full attention.
- The lights are on but nobody's home.
- Big power surges knock them out for the night.
- Size does matter.
- They're heavily dependant on external tools and equipment.
- They periodically cut you off when you think you've
  established a network connection.

If blokes had PMS, what would happen?

The Government would allocate funds to study it.

•

Cramps would become an acceptable reason to apply for permanent disability.

•

There would be a bank holiday every 28 days.

•

All of the above.

Why blokes like e-mail

(clue: it's because it's like a penis)

- In the not-too-distant past, it was just a way to transmit information considered vital to the survival of the species. Now it's just used for fun.
- Once they've started playing with it, it's hard to stop.
- It can be up or down. It's more fun when it's up but it makes it hard to get any real work done.
- It provides a way to interact with people.
- Those who have it would be devastated if it were cut off.
- It has no conscience and no memory. Left to its own devices, it'll do the same dumb things it did before.
- If they're not careful what they do with it, it can land them in big trouble.

Cutting put-downs for blokes who really deserve them

- 'You're like my blender – I wanted it at the time, but I can't remember why.'
- 'I'll see you in my dreams… if I eat too much cheese.'
- 'There was something I liked about you… but the thing is, you've spent it now.'
- 'Darling, no one could love you as much as you do.'
- 'Sleeping with you has made me realise how much I miss my ex.'
- 'It's a shame your parents didn't practise safe sex.'
- 'You're proof enough that I can take a joke.'
- 'The only thing you could be committed to is a mental institution.'

How to impress a woman

- Love her.
- Comfort her.
- Cherish her.
- Protect her.
- Kiss her.
- Cuddle her.
- Listen to her.
- Support her.
- Compliment her.
- Respect her.
- Care for her.

How to impress a bloke:

- Show up naked.
- Bring beer.

Show up naked, bring beer

What to say to annoying blokes who ask: 'Why aren't you married yet?'

- 'What? And spoil my great sex life?'
- 'Just lucky, I guess.'
- 'I wouldn't want my parents to drop dead from sheer happiness.'
- 'We really want to, but my lover's wife just won't go for it.'
- 'I'm waiting till I get to your age.'
- 'My fiancé is waiting for his parole.'
- 'What? And share my trust fund millions?'

Why Santa can't possibly be a bloke.

- Blokes can't pack a bag.
- Most blokes would die rather than be seen wearing red velvet.
- Blokes don't answer letters.
- Blokes aren't interested in stockings unless someone's wearing them.
- The 'ho, ho, ho' thing would seriously inhibit a bloke's pulling power.
- Being totally responsible for Christmas would require commitment.

The medical-sounding notice that might just stop your bloke rolling in drunk at 3 a.m. talking shite.

WARNING: Consumption of alcohol ...

- ...may make you think you're whispering when you're not.
- ...may cause you to thay shings like thish.
- ...may lead you to believe that ex-lovers are dying for you to phone them at 4 a.m.
- ...may leave you wondering what the hell happened to your trousers.
- ...may make you think you do indeed have mystical Kung Fu powers.
- ...is the leading cause of inexplicable carpet burns on your forehead.
- ...may create the illusion that you're tougher, handsomer and smarter than some really, really big bloke called Baz.
- ...may cause a glitch in the space/time continuum, whereby small (and large) gaps of time disappear.
- ...may actually cause pregnancy.
- ...may make you think you can logically converse with members of the opposite sex without spitting.
- ...may cause you to roll over in the morning and see something really scary (whose species and/or name you can't remember.
- ...may lead you to think people are laughing with you, not at you.

Harsh things a woman can say to a naked bloke...

Wow...and your feet are so big!

•

I guess this makes me the early bird!

•

But it still works – right?

•

Are you cold?

•

Maybe if we water it, it'll grow.

•

Why don't we just cuddle?

•

You know they have surgery to fix that.

•

Why is God punishing me?

•

I never saw one like that before.

•

Maybe it looks better in natural light?

Wow…and your feet are so big!

GREAT MYSTERIES OF OUR TIME (I)... WHY?

Why is a **computer** like a **penis**?

If you don't apply the appropriate protective measures,

it can spread viruses.

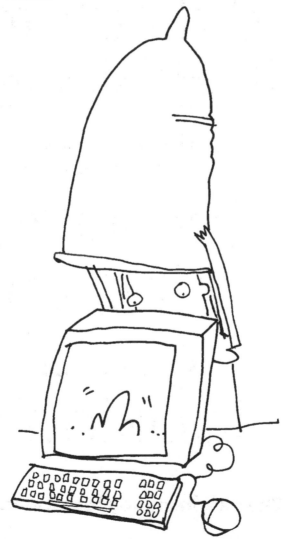

Why is it difficult to find blokes who are sensitive, caring and good looking?

They all have boyfriends already.

Why do blokes like masturbation?

Because it's sex with someone they love.

Why did the man cross the road?

He heard the chicken was a slut.

Why don't women blink during foreplay?

They don't have time.

Why do black widow spiders kill their males after mating?

To stop the snoring before it starts.

Why is sleeping with a bloke like a soap opera?

Just when it's getting interesting,
they're finished until next time.

Why do blokes have a penis and a brain?

No one knows – there isn't enough blood to supply
both at the same time.

Why should you never let your bloke's mind wander?

Because it's too little to be let out alone.

Why do **blokes** find it **difficult** to make **eye contact**?

Breasts don't have eyes.

Why will a woman rarely make a fool of a man?

Most of them are the do-it-yourself types.

Why go for younger men?

You might as well – they never mature anyway.

Why should you never worry about doing housework?

No bloke ever made love to a woman
because the house was spotless?

Why do blokes name their penises?

Because they wouldn't trust a stranger with
90% of their decisions.

Why are all dumb blonde jokes one-liners?

So blokes can remember them.

Why is a bloke's penis like the Rubik's cube?

The more you play with it the harder it gets.

Why is it that a single woman doesn't fart?

She doesn't get an asshole till she gets married.

Why are **women** so **bad** at **mathematics**?

Because blokes keep telling them that

this I--------I is 12 inches.

Why is it good that there are women astronauts?

So that when the crew gets lost in space, at least the women will ask for directions.

Why don't blokes often show their true feelings?

Because they don't have feelings.

Why would women be better off if blokes treated them like cars?

At least then they would get a little attention every 6 months or 5,000 miles, whichever came first.

Why do doctors slap babies' bums right after they're born?

To knock the penises off the clever ones.

Why is food better than men?

Because you don't have to wait an hour for seconds.

Why do blokes like BMWs?

They can spell it.

Why do blokes have a hole in their penis?

So they can get air to their brain.

Why do blokes have their best ideas during sex?

Because they're plugged into a genius!

Why did the man cross the road?
Because he got his knob stuck in the chicken!

Why do blokes always look stupid?
Because they are stupid.

Why did the man cross the road?
Never mind that! What's he doing out of the kitchen!!

Why is psychoanalysis quicker for blokes than for women?
When it's time to go back to childhood,
they're already there.

Why do only 10% of blokes go to heaven?
Because if there were any more it would be hell.

Why do blokes hate wearing condoms?
It cuts off the circulation to their brain.

Why can't **blokes** make **pancakes**?

Because they're useless tossers!

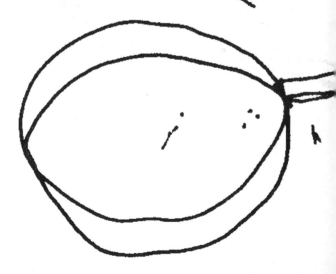

Why do women rub their eyes when they wake up?
Because they don't have balls to scratch.

Why is wee yellow and sperm white?
So a bloke can tell if he's coming or going.

Why did the condom go flying across the room?
It was pissed off.

Why shouldn't you chain a bloke to the sink?
He won't be able to reach the ironing.

Why do women fake orgasms?
Because blokes fake foreplay!

Why do blokes go bald?
To stop them having any more crap hair cuts!!!

Why do blokes buy electric lawnmowers?
So they can find their way back to the house.

Why don't blokes use toilet paper?

Because God made them perfect arses!

4

IF YOU CALL A SPADE A SPADE, WHAT DO YOU CALL A BLOKE....

What do you **call** a **handcuffed bloke**?

Trustworthy.

What do you call a bloke with 90% of his intelligence gone?

Divorced.

What do you call a bloke who expects sex on the second date?

Slow.

What do you call a woman who does the same amount of work as a bloke?

A lazy cow.

What do you call a bloke with half a brain?

Gifted.

What do you call 200 blokes at the bottom of the sea?

A good start.

What do you call a woman who knows where her husband is every night?

A widow.

What do you call a bloke with 99% of his brain missing?

Castrated.

What do you call 144 blokes in a room?

Gross stupidity.

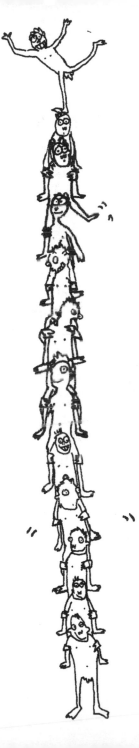

What do you call **twelve naked blokes**, sitting on each other's **shoulders**?

A scrotum pole.

What do you call a woman without an arse?
Single.

What do you call the useless flap of skin on the end of a penis?
A bloke!

What do you call a musician without a girlfriend?
Homeless.

5

IT'S A BIBLE THING!

How do we know **God** is a **man**?

Because if God were a woman, sperm would taste like chocolate.

On the day the good Lord was handing out sex lives, he gave man 20 years of a normal sex life and man protested very loudly. The Lord then gave the monkey 20 years, but the monkey said: 'Lord, 20 years is too much, I only need 10.' Man was standing nearby and overheard. He said to the monkey: 'Can I have the other 10?' and the monkey agreed. Then it was the lion's turn and the Lord also gave the lion 20 years, but the lion assured the Lord he too only needed 10. Man again jumped in and asked for the other 10 and the lion agreed. It was then the donkey's turn and the Lord also gave him 20 years, but he too stated he only needed 10 and of course man requested the donkey's remaining 10 which he got. That explains why blokes spend 20 years having a normal sex life, the next 10 years monkeying around, then the next 10 years lying about, and the last 10 years making asses of themselves.

Why did God make man before woman?

You need a rough draft before you make a final copy.

On the eighth day God was looking down over his creation when he spotted Adam and Eve in the Garden of Eden.

He says to them: 'I've got a couple of leftovers which I might as well hand out to you. I can't decide who should have what, so the person who shouts loudest gets the first choice. The first item is a thing that allows you to pee standing up.'

Adam immediately jumps up and down shouting: 'Me, me, I want that.' So God gives it to him.

'Damn,' thinks Eve. 'That sounds really good. I should have shouted louder.'

'Oh well,' says God. 'I'm afraid all I have left is this multiple orgasm.'

Bill Clinton and the Pope died on the same day but there was a mix-up and Bill Clinton went to Heaven and the Pope went to Hell. The Devil was well pissed off because he wanted to tell Bill Clinton jokes about shagging secretaries. So he phones up God and tells him that they'd better swap the Pope and Bill around. The next day they pass each other and the Pope says to Bill: 'I'm so glad I'm finally going to Heaven. I can't wait to meet the Virgin Mary.' And Bill Clinton says: 'Oops!!!'

Why was **Moses** wandering **through** the desert for **40 years**?

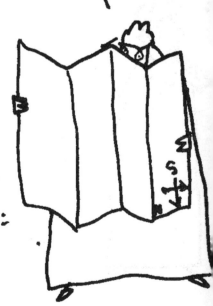

**Because blokes refuse
to ask for directions!**

Three blokes arrive at the gates of Heaven, and are greeted by St Peter. He says to the first man: 'Have you been a good person?' The first man replies: 'Yes, I've led a truly worthwhile life, and I've never been unfaithful to my wife.' So St Peter gives him a Rolls Royce car to aid his travels in Heaven.

Then St Peter asks the second man if he's led a good life. The second man replies: 'Well, mostly I've been honest and caring, but I have been unfaithful to my wife once.'

'Very well,' replies St Peter. 'You may have a Ford Fiesta.'

He goes to the third man and asks him the same question, to which the man replies: 'Well, no. I've stolen from my loved ones, and I've not been faithful to my wife for more than a week.' So St Peter gives the third man a bicycle.

A few days later, the second man and the third

man pass the first man, who's in his gleaming Rolls Royce, sobbing his heart out. The second man asks him: 'What's the matter? If I had your car I'd be the happiest man here!'

'I was,' he replies, 'but I've just seen my wife, and she was on roller-skates.'

What did God say after creating man?

I must be able to do better than that.

C ontrary to the teachings of the Bible, God created Eve first. She was intelligent, beautiful and interesting... and had three breasts! After a few days God came to check on her and she complained that the third breast was a bit uncomfortable, so he said: 'OK we'll throw one away.' This made Eve happy.

Over the next few months she wandered around seeing other animals strolling around in twos and said: 'God, I feel lonely. I need a man.' And God said: 'No problem. Tell me now, where did I throw that useless tit?'

The Lad's Prayer.

Our beer

Which art in barrels

Hallowed be thy drink

Thy will be drunk

I will be drunk

At home as it is in the local

Forgive us this day our daily spillage

As we forgive those that spillest against us

And lead us not into the poncey practise of wine tasting

And deliver us from alco-pops

For mine is the bitter

The ale and the lager

For ever and ever

Barmen.

Why did **God** put **blokes** on **Earth**?

Because a vibrator can't mow the lawn.

6

GREAT MYSTERIES OF OUR TIME (II) ...WHAT'S ALL THAT ABOUT?

What do you **instantly know** about a **well-dressed bloke**?

His wife is good at picking out clothes.

What part of a bloke grows, the more you stroke it?

His ego.

What do electric trains and breasts have in common?

They're intended for children, but it's blokes who usually end up playing with them.

What do blokes consider house cleaning?

Lifting their feet so you can vacuum under them.

What have you got if you have 100 blokes buried up to their necks in sand?
Not enough sand.

What's a bloke's idea of a romantic evening out?
A candlelit football stadium.

What are a woman's four favourite animals?
A mink in the wardrobe, a Jaguar in the garage, a tiger in the bedroom and an ass who'll pay for it all.

What do you have when you've got two little balls in your hand?
A bloke's undivided attention.

What's the best way to get a bloke to do something?
Suggest he's too old for it.

What is the one thing that all blokes at singles bars have in common?
They're married.

What should you do if your **bloke walks out**?

Shut the door after him.

What is a **bloke's** view of **safe sex**?

A padded headboard.

What's the only time a bloke thinks about a candlelit dinner?

When the power goes off.

What's the definition of a bachelor?

A bloke who's missed the opportunity
to make a woman miserable.

What's a bloke's idea of foreplay?

Half an hour of begging.

What's the best time to try and change a bloke?

When he's in nappies.

What should you **reply** if a **bloke** asks you: '**Am I your first?**'

'You could be, you look familiar.'

What are the two reasons blokes don't mind their own business?

i) No mind. ii) No business.

What's the best thing to come out of a penis when you stroke it?

The wrinkles.

What are the measurements of the perfect husband?

82-20-45. That's 82 years old, £20 million in the bank and a 45-degree fever.

What's a world without blokes?

A world full of fat, happy women.

What does a **bloke** consider a **seven course meal**?

A hot dog and a six-pack of beer.

What do **fat blokes** and **mopeds** have in **common**?

**They're both a good ride, but you'd die
if your mates saw you on one!**

What does the smart bloke do in an M&M factory?

Proofread.

What's the **thinnest** book in the **world**?

What Blokes Know About Women.

What's a bloke's definition of a romantic evening?

Sex.

What do a **clitoris**, an **anniversary**, and a **toilet** have in **common**?

Blokes always miss them.

What does a bloke have to do to keep you interested in his company?

Own it!

What does a **girl** have to say to **seduce** a **bloke**?

'Hi.'

7

SO THIS BLOKE GOES INTO A PUB...

A bloke goes into a supermarket and buys a tube of toothpaste, a bottle of Pepsi, a bag of tortilla chips, and a frozen pizza. The cute girl at the register looks at him and says: 'Single, huh?' Sarcastically the bloke sneers: 'How'd you guess?' She replies: 'Because you're ugly.'

A bloke staggers home at 3 a.m. after a pub-crawl. On finding his wife awake and naked in bed he decides to show some interest. He gently kisses her on the forehead but no response.

He then softly kisses her lips still no response. Moving downwards he caresses her neck and then brushes his lips expertly across each breast, before continuing slowly downward with his tongue until it finds a haven exploring her navel. No reaction whatsoever. His next move is to bend right down and kiss inside her right thigh just above her knee. At that moment his wife sits bolt upright and screams: 'If it had been a pub you wouldn't have missed it!'

A bloke was trying to decide which of three women he would ask to marry him. He gave them each £1000.

The first spent £900 on clothes, and put £100 in the bank.

The second spent £500 on clothes and put £500 in the bank.

The third spent £100 on clothes and put £900 in the bank.

Which one did he choose?

The one with the big breasts.

A bloke goes to the doctors and says:

'Doctor, doctor, you've got to help me. I've got six willies!'

The doctor looks at him in disbelief:

'That's a load of bollocks!!'

Two women are talking on the phone.
One says to the other:

'Hang on a minute, the old man popped down the garden ages ago to get a cabbage for dinner and he's not come back. I'd better look for him.'

When she comes back to the phone she says:

'Oh no! He's dropped dead in the vegetable patch.'

'What are you going to do now?' her friend replies. Quick as a flash she says: 'Damn. I'll have to open a tin of peas!'

A woman goes into a card shop and stands for a long time staring at the specialist cards, finally shaking her head,

'No.' Eventually a shop assistant comes over and asks if he can help.

'I don't know,' said the woman. 'Do you have any "Sorry I laughed at your dick" cards?'

Three blokes are discussing the control they have over their wives.

The first bloke says: 'I have immense control over my wife. Every night I come home from work to find my dinner waiting for me on the table.'

The second bloke says: 'I have total control over my wife. Every night I come home from work to find a hot bath ready and waiting.'

The third bloke says: 'The other night, lads, my wife came to me on her hands and knees.'

The other two are really impressed with this and ask: 'Yeah? what did she say?'

'GET OUT FROM UNDER THAT BED AND FIGHT LIKE A MAN!!!'

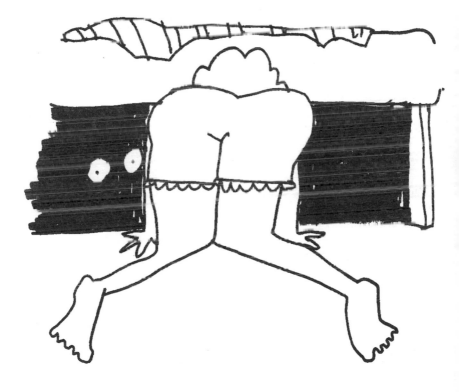

A woman goes into a shop to buy a wedding dress – for her fourth wedding. She chooses a traditional white dress, which surprises the sales assistant.

'Oh but I'm still a virgin,' the woman replies.

'How can that be,' says the sales assistant, 'if this is to be your fourth wedding.'

'My first husband was a psychologist he just wanted to talk about it; my second husband was a gynaecologist he just wanted to look at it; my third husband was a stamp collector... God I loved him!'

A nun walks onto a bus, which is empty except for the driver. The nun says to the driver: 'I'm going to die soon but I want three wishes fulfilled before I do. Firstly, I want to have sex, but I must die a virgin, so the sex has to be anal. Secondly, I cannot commit adultery, so the bloke I sleep with has to be single. Finally, the bloke has to be a stranger to me and must not tell anyone else.'

The nun then asks the bus driver if he thinks he's up to fulfilling the wishes.

The bus driver readily agrees and takes the nun upstairs, promptly fulfilling the first wish, but afterwards he feels very guilty and says to the nun: 'I'm afraid I've lied to you, I am in fact married with three children.'

The nun replies: 'That's OK, I've lied too. My name's Kevin and I'm off to a fancy dress party!'

A bloke goes to see his doctor for a check-up. During the examination the doctor notices the bloke's yellow penis. The doctor asks him a few questions. 'Do you work with chemicals, young man?'

'No,' replies the bloke, 'I'm unemployed.'

'Well do you smoke?' asks the doctor.

'No, I don't smoke,' says the bloke.

By now the doctor is a bit perplexed. 'But how did you get a yellow penis, then?'

'I dunno,' replies the man. 'I just sit at home all day, watching porno videos and eating cheesy puffs.'

A bloke picks up a female partner at the golf club. She cleans him out, and as compensation takes him home and gives him the mother and father of all blowjobs. He's so pleased that he asks for a return match and the same thing happens several times.

Next time, he suggests they have full sex, but she admits that she's actually a bloke in the process of a sex change. When he goes wild, the transsexual asks why he's so angry when he clearly enjoyed the blowjobs.

The bloke replies: 'Never mind the blowjobs. You've been playing off the ladies' tees!'

A bloke and a woman are strolling down a beach on a romantic moonlit night. Gently the bloke takes the woman's hand and asks her to close her eyes. He then places her hand on his crotch. To which she retorts: 'No thanks, I don't smoke.'

Two sperm are swimming along happily. One sperm says to the other. 'How much further have we got to swim before we get to that egg?'

'I dunno, mate,' says the other sperm. 'We've only just passed the tonsils.'

A bloke is driving up a steep, narrow mountain road. A woman is driving down the same road. As they pass each other, the woman leans out of the window and yells: 'PIG!!' The bloke immediately leans out of his window and replies: 'BITCH!!' They each continue on their way, and as the bloke rounds the next corner, he crashes into a pig in the middle of the road. If only blokes would listen.

A bloke walks into a pub and asks the barman for six double whiskies. The Barman looks shocked: 'Six double whiskies, that's an awful lot for someone who's come in on his own!'

'But I've just had my first blowjob,' replies the man.

'In that case have another one on the house,' states the barman. 'Well,' says the bloke, 'If six doesn't take the taste away, I don't think seven will!'

A couple are having a blazing row, and things are starting to get personal. 'I don't know why you wear a bra,' says the bloke. 'You haven't got anything to put in there!' The woman stares at him in disbelief: 'Well you wear pants, don't you?'

A bloke walks into a bar, and says to the barman: 'I'd like an orange juice please.'

The barman says: 'Still?'

The bloke says: 'Well I haven't changed my fucking mind!'

An intelligent woman, an intelligent bloke and the tooth fairy were walking down the road one day when they looked down and noticed a £5 note on the pavement. Which one picked the £5 note up?

The intelligent woman of course… the other two don't exist!

8

WHAT ARE
THEY LIKE?!

Why are blokes like floor tiles?

Lay them right the first time, and you can walk all over them for the rest of your life!

Why are **boring blokes** like **snot**?

They get up your nose.

Why are **blokes** like **cool bags**?

Load them with beer and you can take them anywhere.

Why are blokes like high heels?

They're easy to walk on once you get the hang of it.

Why are **blokes** like **horoscopes**?

They always tell you what to do and are usually wrong.

Why are blokes like bank accounts?

Without a lot of money, they don't generate much interest.

Why are **blokes** like lawn **mowers**?

If you're not pushing one around, then you're riding it.

Why are blokes like used cars?

Both are easy-to-get, cheap, and unreliable.

Why are **blokes** like **chocolate bars**?

They're sweet, smooth, and they usually head right for your hips.

Why are **blokes** like **holidays**?

They never seem to be long enough.

Why are blokes like mascara?

They usually run at the first sign of emotion.

Why are **blokes** like **place-mats**?

They only show up when there's food on the table.

Why are blokes like lava lamps?

Fun to look at, but not all that bright.

Why are blokes like cement?

After getting laid, they take a long time to get hard.

Why are blokes like plungers?

**They spend most of
their lives in a hardware store
or the bathroom.**

Why are **blokes** like **blenders**?

You need one, but you don't know why.

Why are blokes like toilets?

Because they're always either engaged, vacant or full of crap.

Why are **blokes** like **beer bottles**?

Because they're both empty from the neck up!

Why are blokes like popcorn?

They satisfy you, but only for a little while.

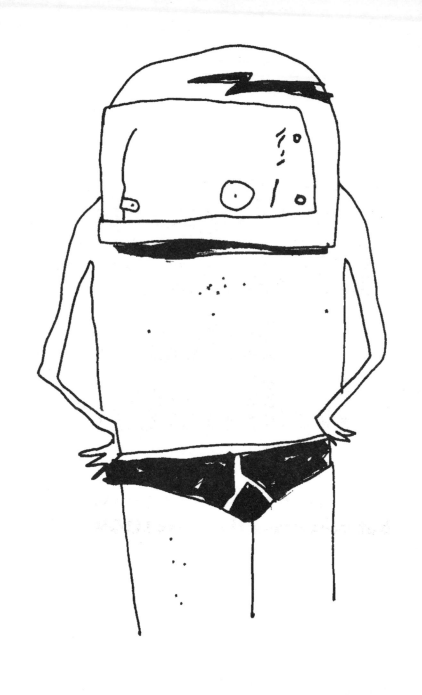

Why are **blokes** like **bike helmets**?

**Handy in an emergency,
but otherwise they just LOOK SILLY.**

Why are **blokes** like **parking spaces**?

Because the good ones are always gone and the only ones left are disabled.

Why are blokes like coffee?

The best ones are rich, warm, and can keep you up all night long.

Why are **blokes** like **spray paint**?

One squeeze and they're all over you.

Why are blokes like cashpoint machines?

Once they withdraw they lose interest.

Why are blokes like like caravans?

Because they follow wherever you take them.

Why are **blokes** like **laxatives**?

They both irritate the shit out of you.

Why are blokes like sperms?

They both have only a one in a million chance of becoming a human being.

Why are **blokes** like **computers**?

You never know how much they mean to you until they go down on you.

Why are blokes like a snowstorm?

'Cos you don't know when they're coming, how long they're going to last or how many inches you'll get!

Why are **blokes** like **department stores**?

Their clothes should always be half off.

Why are blokes like dog poos?

The older they get the easier they are to pick up!

9

GREAT MYSTERIES OF OUR TIME (III) ... HOW COME?

How do you drown a muscle man?

You put a mirror in a pool!

How can you tell the difference between blokes' real gifts and their guilt gifts?

Guilt gifts are nicer.

How many **blokes** does it **take** to change a **toilet roll**?

Who knows, it hasn't happened yet!

How are blokes like noodles?
They're always in hot water, they lack taste,
and they need dough.

How can you **keep** a **bloke happy**?
Who cares?

How many blokes does it take to tile a bathroom?
One – if you slice him thinly enough.

How many **blokes** does it take to **screw** in a **lightbulb**?
One... men will screw anything.

How come blokes have such small balls?
Because so very few of them can dance.

How do you stop a bloke from drowning?

Take your foot off his head.

How do you get a **bloke** to do **sit-ups**?

Put the remote control between his toes.

How can you tell if a bloke is well-hung?

You can't get your finger between the rope and his neck.

How do you know when a **bloke** is **gonna** say **something clever**?

He starts off with 'My girlfriend says...

How many blokes does it take to change a lightbulb?

Three. One to change it, and two to listen while he brags about how he screwed it...

How do you know when your **bloke** is getting **old**?

When he starts having dry dreams and wet farts.

How many blokes does it take to change a lightbulb?

One. He just holds it there and waits for the world to revolve around him.

How does a **bloke** take a **bubble bath**?

He eats beans for dinner.

How does a bloke's mind work?
It doesn't… it's always on sick leave!

How do you know when a bloke is lying?

His lips move.

How is a bloke like the weather?

Nothing can be done to change either one of them.

How can you **tell** if a **bloke** is **excited**?

He's breathing.

How can you grow your own dope?

Bury a bloke and wait till spring.

How does a **bloke** get air to his **brain**?

He opens his flies.

How many blokes does it take to pop popcorn?

Three. One to hold the pan and two others to show off and shake the stove.

How does a **bloke** keep a **woman** **screaming** after **climax**?

He wipes his willy on the curtains!

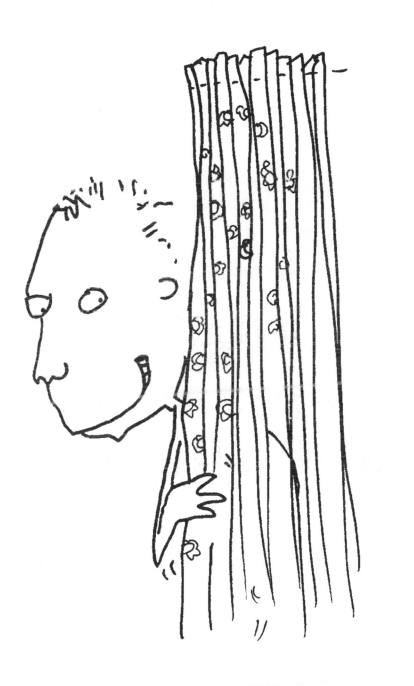

How can you find a committed bloke?

Look in a mental institution.

How many **divorced blokes** does it **take** to change a **lightbulb**?

Nobody knows, they never get the house!

How do blokes extend the washing life of their boxer shorts?

They turn them inside out.

How should you **reply** to a **bloke** who says: **'Hey, you're just my type**.'?

'I think you must be mistaken – I have a pulse.'

How do you stop a lust-filled bloke?

Marry him.

How can a bloke tell when a woman has had a good orgasm?

When the buzzing of her vibrator stops.

How could you **spot the blokes** who **stole** a job lot of **Viagra**?

They're a bunch of hardened criminals in possession of swollen goods.

How many honest, caring, intelligent blokes does it take to do the washing-up?

Both of them.

How do you know if a **bloke's** been in your **garden**?

Your bins have been knocked over and your dog is pregnant.

How can you **spot a man** with **five willies**?

His underpants fit like a glove!

How do **blokes exercise** on the **beach**?

By sucking in their stomach every time a bikini goes by.